the Journey

Quotes to keep
your boat afloat!

from Judy Suiter

Competitive Edge, Inc.
P.O. Box 2418 • Peachtree City, GA 30269
www.competitiveedgeinc.com

The Journey: Quotes To Keep Your Boat Afloat

Copyright 2005 by Judy Suiter

Published by Competitive Edge, Inc.

Design, illustrations and typography by Chris Carey

Photographs by Tim Burgess and Istockphoto.com

Cover photograph by Tim Burgess

Disclaimer: The purpose of this book is to provide insights regarding motivation, personal improvement, and relationship skills. It is not meant to replace professional counsel for legal or financial matters, or for emotional or psychological issues. Referral to a competent business consultant, or to a qualified counselor or therapist, is recommended for use outside the scope of this publication, which is intended for general use and not as a specific course of treatment.

ISBN 0-9721790-3-8

Printed in U.S.A.

First Edition – February, 2005
Second Edition – January, 2006

Special appreciation to photographer Tim Burgess, whose images fill this book and grace the cover.

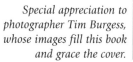

Dedication

I dedicate this book to my mother, the late Lois Irene
Bohlke, who was not only my inspiration but my best friend.

Acknowledgments

Friends suggested that I compile a book featuring some of the meaningful quotations I use in my seminars. Quotations are not random thoughts. They are words and ideas someone expressed in the past, meaningful enough for others to recall, apply and pass on. I selected these quotations with the desire that they will serve you well. So, I begin by acknowledging those who encouraged me to do this.

It was my friend of 26 years, Janet Boyce, who came up with the book's nautical journey theme. A strong encourager, she helped me organize the quotes into categories. Space doesn't permit me to share stories of other friends and our intertwined lives, but *we* know what they are, and here are their names:

Jack Gilpin, Judy Murray, Lee and Hal Murray, Lil Sauer, Betty Spradling, Eleonore and Al Walters, all friends from the 70s in Smyrna, Tennessee, who continue to offer friendship and support.

Bob Anderson, Dr. Jack Charlesworth, Dr. Vikki Ashley, Jan Eley, the late Pete George, H.R. "Hap" Hannon (who gave me my first training job in 1982), Jim Kerr, Michelle Lee, Katherine Simons, Barbara and Bill Strickland.

Our history is not as long, but our bond is strong: Vijay Anand, Joan Bendetti, Ida Bowen, Vickie Burns, Chris Carey, Karen Chapman, Tom Cherry, Elinor Colby, Tommy Curtis, Nancy Deane, Joe Dixon, Diane Evans, Rebecca Franklin, Alice Haslam, Christiane Hoffmann, Hank Humphry, Amy Jones, Joe Kearns, Jim Larson, Joe Miller, Carol Moser, Jerry Nagel, Jennifer Peterson, Shirley Richard, Cindy Rightmyer, Steve Saenz, Annette Segil, Krista Sheets, Ed Shipley, Erica Smith, and David Swindle.

Thank you all for being part of my life.

A Note to My Readers

Twenty-some years ago, I knew that it was time to make significant changes in my life. What has occurred over the intervening decades has been so remarkable that I can honestly say that, despite many difficulties, hardships and losses, it has been a wonderful journey.

So, as I put together this book of quotes for you, I decided to organize it along the lines of taking a journey, sailing across the oceans to a new destination.

As you know, making a successful journey requires a great deal of foresight. Likewise, this book is designed to take you from the initial planning stage to the point where you come ashore at your new and exciting future.

You will experience the characteristics of ocean sailing, including heavy weather, storms, incredible calm and time for reflection as you travel to your destination. Bear in mind the words of Leonardo da Vinci: "He turns not back who is bound to a star."

For your journey, I wish you Godspeed.

Table of Contents

WINDS OF CHANGE

Change: *to cause to become different, alter; convert; to pass from one phase to another.*

Part 1: Winds of Change

Just as is the weather, we are impacted by the wind. Its direction is never steady and, just as the weather changes, we do also through times of turbulence and calm. All of a sudden, what we have been doing for so long no longer makes sense; we begin to sway with the winds of change and thus, we begin a new journey, an awakening of sorts.

Before this new experience can commence, we must make certain that we can adjust our sails for the trip. This calls for a pre-departure checklist, ensuring that we are following the right wind. Read the words of philosopher Marcus Annaeus Stone:

> **"Our plans miscarry because they have no aim. When a man does not know what harbor he is making for, no wind is the right wind."**

So, we have some work to do before we set sail. We need to take inventory of who we are, what we want, which talents and shortcomings we possess, in order to make certain that we are following the right wind. In other words, we are seeking to better know ourselves before shoving off to our next port of call. As Andre Gide writes:

> **"It is only in adventure that some people succeed in knowing themselves—in finding themselves."**

As we acquiesce to the winds of change, let's begin our preparation by looking at change: what it means and how we view it.

Change

"The journey of a thousand miles begins with a single step." — *Chinese Proverb*

"Life is either a daring adventure or nothing at all." — *Helen Keller*

"We cannot become what we need to be by remaining what we are." — *Max DePree*

"You can't change what you won't acknowledge." — *Phil McGraw*

"Be the change that you want to see in the world." – *Mohandas K. Gandhi*

"When you're through changing, you're through." — *Bruce Barton*

"For a long time it had seemed to me that life was about to be — real life, but there was always some obstacle in the way; something to be worked through first, some unfinished business, time still to be served, a debt to be paid. Then life would begin. At last it dawned on me that these obstacles were my life." — *Alfred D. Souza*

"Either you decide to stay in the shallow end of the pool or you go out in the ocean." — *Christopher Reeve*

"Change is what people fear most." — *Fyodor Dostoyevsky*

"You must change in order to survive." — *Pearl Bailey*

"Change is good ... You go first. " — *Dilbert*

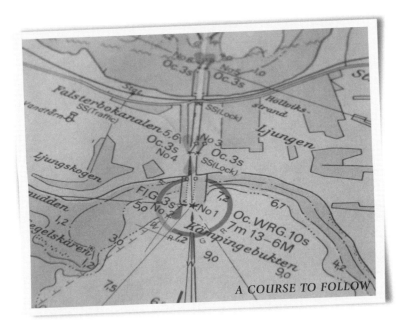

A COURSE TO FOLLOW

Charting Your Course

Preparing for a journey always requires the use of a chart to plot a course. The chart is the navigator's key tool; it is like a guide book loaded with facts to help us pick out known landmarks that will assist in our journey.

We want to highlight those characteristics that we bring with us on this voyage to a new destination. Think of these basic ideals as the underpinnings of our ship, as they will carry us across both calm and stormy waters.

These are the positive aspects that make us who we are, those qualities that keep our ship steady through all types of weather, good and bad. They determine how we react to events in our lives. We are still in the preparation phase of our journey, and as I promised, it does take some time.

GETTING READY

Preparation: *the act of setting or placing in order;*
getting ready. Equipping or furnishing with
necessary provisions, accessories, etc., fitting out as
for an expedition.

Part 2: Getting Ready

We now turn to the preparation phase of our journey, in which we will examine our strengths, our purposes and our shortcomings.

During our journey, it is certain that we will be tried as never before. Our fundamental moorings will be challenged, and survival will depend upon those truths, beliefs and skills that have brought us to this point in life.

The preparation process can be lengthy and, at times quite painful, as we attempt to pack our bags. Some of our baggage must be left behind, as the weight of some experiences and past events will serve only to slow us down, hampering not only our progress, but also our future endeavors.

An old Arabic proverb warns us:

"Think of the going out before you enter."

Remember, the key to a successful journey is in the preparation.

Preparation

"If you don't have a plan for yourself, you'll be part of someone else's." — *American Proverb*

"Investment always precedes return." — *Unknown*

"Make no little plans; they have no magic to stir men's blood and probably will themselves not be realized. Make big plans; aim high in hope and work, remembering that a noble, logical diagram once recorded will not die." — *Daniel H. Burnham*

"Failing to plan is planning to fail." — *Alan Lakein*

"It pays to plan ahead. It wasn't raining when Noah built the ark." — *Unknown*

"Expect the best, plan for the worst, and prepare to be surprised." — *Denis Waitley*

"If you aren't prepared, don't expect to win." — *Coach Paul "Bear" Bryant*

"To be prepared is half the victory." — *Miguel de Cervantes*

"To accomplish great things, we must not only act, but also dream; not only plan, but also believe." — *Anatole France*

"People only see what they are prepared to see." — *Ralph Waldo Emerson*

"Luck is a matter of preparation meeting opportunity." — *Oprah Winfrey*

Discovering Our Strengths

"If you do not ask yourself what it is you know, you will go on listening to others and change will not come because you will not hear your own truth."
— *St. Bartholomew*

"I think self-awareness is probably the most important thing towards becoming a champion." — *Billie Jean King*

"He who knows others is learned. He who knows himself is wise."
— *Lao Tsu*

"If you know the enemy and know yourself, you need not fear the result of a hundred battles. If you know yourself but not the enemy, for every victory gained, you will also suffer a defeat. If you know neither the enemy nor yourself, you will succumb in every battle."
– *Sun Tsu*

"There are three things extremely hard: steel, diamonds, and to know oneself." — *Benjamin Franklin*

"You don't get to choose how you're going to die. Or when. You can only decide how you're going to live."
— *Joan Baez*

"You never find yourself until you face the truth."
— *Pearl Bailey*

"You must do the thing you think you cannot do."
— *Eleanor Roosevelt*

"In order to understand our relationships with other people, we must first understand ourselves."
— *Bill J. Bonnstetter*

"If you aren't getting faster, stronger and smarter, you are getting slower, weaker and dumber."

— *Veronica Ross*

"If you think you're too small to have an impact, try going to bed with a mosquito in the room."

— *Anita Roddick*

"We see ourselves in light of our intentions and others see us by observing our actions." — *Dr. Michael O'Connor*

"What do you know for sure?" — *Oprah Winfrey*

"Seek first to understand and then to be understood."

— *Stephen Covey*

UNDERPINNINGS

Underpinnings: *that which supports or holds up.*

Positive Thinking

"Man is what he believes."   — *Anton Chekhov*

"Everything can be taken from a man but one thing: the last of the human freedoms — to choose one's attitude in any given set of circumstances, to choose one's own way."   — *Viktor Frankl*

"The greatest discovery of my generation is that man can alter his life simply by altering his attitude of mind."   — *William James*

"Success is not a place at which one arrives, but rather the spirit with which one undertakes and continues the journey."   — *Alex Noble*

"Do what you can, with what you have, where you are."   — *Theodore Roosevelt*

"Ninety percent of life is showing up."   — *Woody Allen*

"To accomplish great things, we must not only act, but also dream; not only plan, but also believe."   — *Anatole France*

"Ability is what you're capable of doing. Motivation determines what you do. Attitude determines how well you do it."   — *Lou Holtz*

"A great attitude makes you feel like you are rowing with the current instead of against it."   — *Earl Suttle, Ph.D.*

"Misery is optional; it is not a by-product of living."   — *Pamela Cole*

"History is full of examples of giants, like the dinosaurs, who couldn't adapt."   — *Unknown*

"CHALLENGE: Curiosity, Hindsight, Adaptability, Laughter, Love, Encouragement, Need, Gentleness, Energy."   — *Clair Duggar*

ENTHUSIASM

Enthusiasm

"Enthusiasm is the greatest asset in the world; it beats money, power and influence."   — *Henry Chester*

"Nothing great in the world has been accomplished without passion."   — *George Hegel*

"The essential (conditions) of everything you do must be choice, love, passion."   — *Nadia Boulanger*

"Man is only truly great when he acts from his passions."
— *Benjamin Disraeli*

"Find something you're passionate about and keep tremendously interested in it."
— *Julia Child*

"Winning isn't everything. *Wanting* to win is."
— *Catfish Hunter*

"Work like you don't need money. Love like you've never been hurt. And dance like no one's watching."
— *Irish proverb*

"Never underestimate the power of passion."
— *Eve Sawyer*

Convictions

"I keep my ideals, because in spite of everything I still believe that people are really good at heart."
— *Anne Frank*

"Let us remember that within us there is a palace of immense magnificence."
— *Teresa of Avila*

"The truth of the matter is you always know the right thing to do. The hard part is doing it."
— *General H. Norman Schwarzkopf*

"We can do no great things—only small things with great love."
— *Mother Teresa*

"Truth, like surgery, may hurt, but it cures."
— *Han Suyin*

"It is easier to fight for one's principles than to live up to them." — *Alfred Adler*

"It is only with the heart that one can see rightly... What is essential is invisible." — *The Little Prince*

Forgiveness

"The weak can never forgive. Forgiveness is the attribute of the strong." — *Mohandas K. Gandhi*

"One forgives to the degree that one loves." — *Francois de La Rochefoucauld*

"'I can forgive, but I cannot forget' is only another way of saying, 'I will not forgive.' Forgiveness ought to be like a cancelled note—torn in two and burned up so that it never can be shown against one." — *Henry Ward Beecher*

"Always forgive your enemies; nothing annoys them so much." — *Oscar Wilde*

"To be wronged is nothing unless you continue to remember it." — *Confucius*

"When you harbor bitterness, happiness will dock elsewhere." — *Andy Rooney*

"Friends may come and friends may go, but enemies accumulate." — *Rich Devos*

Values

"It is easier to exemplify values than teach them."
— *Theodore Hesburg*

"On a group of theories one can found a school; but on a group of values one can found a culture, a civilization, a new way of living together among men."
— *Ignazio Silone*

"The most important thing in life is deciding what's most important."
— *Dr. Michael O'Connor*

"Open your arms to change, but don't let go of your values."
— *The Dalai Lama*

"Never sacrifice what you want most for what you want now."
— *Toby Tolbert*

"Everyone's values are defined by what they will tolerate when it is done to others."
— *William Greider*

"We can tell our values by looking at our checkbook stubs."
— *Gloria Steinem*

"How we spend our days is how we spend our lives."
– *Annie Dillard*

"The hero is valorous because he stands up to every threat against his values. Heroism requires values conflict."
— *Andrew Bernstein*

"Life's ups and downs provide windows of opportunity to determine your values and goals—think of using all obstacles as stepping stones to build the life you want."
— *Marsha Sinetar*

"Know yourself, like yourself, be yourself." — *Chuck Swindoll*

Or, as I say every time I teach my course on Values, "If you do not know what your values and life priorities are, someone else will determine them for you."

— *Judy*

VISION

Vision

"The tragedy of life doesn't lie in not reaching your goal. The tragedy lies in having no goal to reach."

— *Benjamin Mays*

"Cherish your visions and your dreams as they are the children of your soul; the blueprints of your ultimate achievements."

— *Napoleon Hill*

"Your vision will become clear only when you look into your heart. Who looks outside, dreams. Who looks inside, wakens." *— Carl Jung*

"You have to have a dream so you can get up in the morning." *—Billy Wilder*

"Reappraise the past, reevaluate where we've been, clarify where we are, and predict or anticipate where we are headed." *— Toni Cade Bambara*

"Vision without action is a daydream. Action without vision is a nightmare." *— Japanese Proverb*

"Do not let your memories be bigger than your dreams." *— Doug McAllister*

"To make a dream come true, you must first have a great dream." *— Hans Selye*

"Man is not limited so much by his tools as by his vision." *— Unknown*

"I think the purpose of life is to be useful, to be responsible, to be honorable, to be compassionate. It is, after all, to matter: to count, to stand for something, to have made some difference that you lived at all." *— Leo C. Rosten*

"It is never too late to be what you might have been." *— George Eliot*

"Don't let anyone steal your dreams. It's your dream, not theirs." *— Don Zadra*

EXCESS BAGGAGE

Excess Baggage: *An overload of unnecessary items.*

Excess Baggage

Our last bit of preparation consists of getting rid of the excess baggage that tends to hinder our going forward.

We all have had our share of anger, failure, losses, disappointments, or misunderstandings; but in moving forward, there is just no room for it. So let's take a look at the negatives we have been harboring for much too long and let them go.

Edith Johnson puts it this way:

"Having harvested all the knowledge and wisdom we can from our mistakes and failures, we should put them behind us and go ahead."

It is time to lighten our load.

Anger

"I can't express anger. I internalize it and grow a tumor instead." — *Woody Allen*

"Anger dies quickly with a good man." — *English Proverb*

"The anger of the prudent never shows." — *Burmese Proverb*

"Anyone can get angry—that is easy...but to do this to the right person, to the right extent, at the right time, with the right motive, and in the right way, that is not for everyone, nor is it easy." — *Aristotle*

"A chip on the shoulder is too heavy a piece of
 baggage to carry through life." — *John Hancock*

"You cannot shake hands with a closed fist."
                                      — *Indira Gandhi*

"Sticks and stones may break our bones, but words
 will break our hearts."   — *Robert Fulghum*

"Anger is the only thing to put off till tomorrow."
                                   — *Slovakian Proverb*

"Anger is really disappointed hope."   — *Erica Jong*

"He who conquers his anger has conquered an
 enemy."   — *German Proverb*

"We all boil at different degrees." — *Ralph Waldo Emerson*

Failure

"We all die, that's no failure. Not living fully is the
 only failure."   — *Bernie S. Siegel, M.D.*

"Fall seven times, get up eight."   — *Japanese Proverb*

"Failure is success if we learn from it."
                                   — *Malcolm S. Forbes*

"Forget your mistakes, but remember what they taught
 you."   — *Dorothy Galyean*

"I would prefer to fail with honor than win by
 cheating."   — *Sophocles*

"The greatest mistake a person can make is to be
afraid of making one."   — *Elbert Hubbard*

"A mistake is simply another way of doing things."
                                        — *Katherine Graham*

"And what if I did run my ship aground; oh, still it was
splendid to sail it!"   — *Henrik Ibsen*

One of my favorite phrases on failure is, "Some
people have never failed at anything, but they have
had many significant learning experiences."   — *Judy*

SPLENDID TO SAIL

Losses, Disappointments and Worry

"You gotta play the hand that's dealt you. There may be pain in that hand, but you play it." — *James Brady*

"If your eyes are blinded with your worries, you cannot see the beauty of the sunset." — *Krishnamurti*

"One cannot get through life without pain...What we can do is choose how to use the pain life presents to us." — *Bernie S. Siegel, M.D.*

"I am reminded of the advice of my neighbor: 'Never worry about your heart 'til it stops beating.'"
  — *E.B. White*

"Sometimes God has to hit our head with a brick to get our attention." — *Veronica Ross*

DREAMS ADRIFT

Fears

"All forms of fear produce fatigue."   — *Bertrand Russell*

"A man who is afraid will do anything."
— *Jawaharlal Nehru*

"Fear is the absence of faith."   — *Paul Tillich*

"When Fear knocked at its door, Faith answered and no one was there."   — *Unknown*

"I wanted to be scared again...I wanted to feel unsure again. That's the only way I learn, the only way I feel challenged."   — *Connie Chung*

"We all fear what we don't know—it's natural."
– *Leo Buscaglia*

"The first and great commandment is, 'Don't let them scare you.'"   — *Elmer Davis*

"No action so effectively robs the mind of powers of acting and reasoning as fear."   — *Edmund Burke*

"FEAR: False Evidence Appearing Real."   — *Unknown*

"When you win, nothing hurts."   — *Joe Namath*

"Procrastination is the fear of success."   — *Denis Waitley*

"Things done well and with care, exempt themselves from fear."   — *William Shakespeare*

GETTING UNDER WAY

Getting Under Way: *The act or process of setting sail.*

Part 3: Getting Under Way

The preparation is finished. We have completed the checklist of those things we need to carry with us, and have once and for all, packed away those things that have caused us pain. The process of getting under way has begun.

Using what we have learned about ourselves and what we are able to see and hear, we are ready to begin the ancient art called piloting, or navigating as it is most commonly known. Read the words of Mark Twain:

> **"Twenty years from now, you will be more disappointed by the things you didn't do than by the ones you did do. So throw off the bowline. Sail away from the safe harbor. Catch the trade winds in your sails. Explore. Dream. Discover."**

Let's stow away our gear and get ready for the time of our lives. As we leave shore, we will look at some of the key elements of navigation so we can get it right.

NAVIGATION

Navigation

Navigation requires many actions and reactions from us. We need to pay careful attention to our chart; we must constantly watch for dangerous currents and obstacles, and we need to move in the correct direction to our destination.

In this next section, we will direct our attention to other tools that can help guide us: the compass we have with us and the buoys and lighthouses that we see along the way. Let me explain how we will use these aids.

Direction

"I find the great thing in this world is not so much where we stand, as in what direction we are moving: To reach the port of heaven, we must sail sometimes with the wind and sometimes against it, but we must sail, and not drift, nor lie at anchor."
— *Oliver Wendell Holmes*

"Go confidently in the direction of your dreams. Live the life you have imagined." — *Henry David Thoreau*

"You have brains in your head. You have feet in your shoes. You can steer yourself in any direction you choose. You're on your own. And you know what you know. And YOU are the one who'll decide where to go." — *Theodor "Dr. Seuss" Geisel*

"People with goals succeed because they know where they are going." — *Earl Nightingale*

"The hardest thing to learn in life is which bridge to cross and which to burn." — *David Russell*

"No wind serves him who addresses his voyage to no certain port." — *Michel de Montaigne*

"When schemes are laid in advance, it is surprising how often the circumstances fit in with them." — *Sir William Osler*

"Do not go where the path may lead; go instead where there is no path and leave a trail." — *Ralph Waldo Emerson*

33

Determination

"Some succeed because they are destined to, but most succeed because they are determined."
— Henry Van Dyke

"Big shots are only little shots who keep shooting."
— Christopher Morley

"The difference between the impossible and the possible lies in a person's determination."
— Tommy Lasorda

"Good things come to those who wait, but great things come to those who hustle."   *— Earl Suttle, Ph.D.*

"If I shoot at the sun, I may hit a star."   *— P.T. Barnum*

"Unless you try to do something beyond what you have already mastered you will never grow."
– Ralph Waldo Emerson

"There is no finish line."   *— Nike Corporation Motto*

"Do not let what you cannot do interfere with what you can do."   *— John Wooden*

"Be Big: Think Big. Act Big. Dream Big."
— Conrad Hilton

Ability

"If we did all the things we are capable of, we would astound ourselves."   *— Thomas Alva Edison*

"Ability is useless unless it's used."   — *Robert Half*

"A's hire A's, B's hire C's."   — *Donald Rumsfeld*

"Any idiot can face a crisis – it's the day-to-day living that wears you out."   — *Anton Chekhov*

"One only gets to the top rung on the ladder by steadily climbing up one at a time, and suddenly, all sorts of powers, all sorts of abilities which you thought never belonged to you—suddenly become within your own possibility and you think, 'Well, I'll have a go, too.'"   — *Margaret Thatcher*

"Don't measure yourself by what you have accomplished, but by what you should have accomplished with your ability."   — *John Wooden*

"A smooth sea never made a skilled mariner."
          — *English Proverb*

"It's not boasting when you deliver."   — *Doug Hall*

"If I had more skill at what I'm attempting, I wouldn't need so much courage."   — *Ashleigh Brilliant*

"Tis skill, not strength, that governs a ship."
          — *Thomas Fuller*

"They are able because they think they are able."
          — *Virgil*

"I hear and I forget. I see and I remember. I do and I understand."   — *Confucius*

COMPASS

Compass

The compass is an instrument for showing direction. Ancient stargazers noticed that one star in the northern sky was constant; it never moved.

Even though your ship is tossed and turned on the oceans, the rotating circular card on the compass always stays firmly aligned with the magnetic north.

At times, you may need to correct your course when lines of position show danger and harm along the way. I like to think of the compass as one's character that always keeps one on a steady course.

Character

"Character cannot be developed in ease and quiet. Only through experience of trial and suffering can the soul be strengthened, vision cleared, ambition inspired, and success achieved." — *Helen Keller*

"Talent develops in tranquility, character in the full current of human life." — *Johann Wolfgang von Goethe*

"Ability may get you to the top, but it takes character to keep you there." — *John Wooden*

"Character is what you know you are, not what others think you have." — *Marva Collins*

"You can tell the true character of a man by the choices he makes under pressure." — *Winston Churchill*

"Never acquire a lifestyle you're willing to sell your soul to keep." — *Johnnetta B. Cole*

"Men acquire a particular quality by constantly acting in a particular way." — *Aristotle*

"Character is power." — *Booker T. Washington*

"Don't compromise yourself. You're all you got." — *Janis Joplin*

"You cannot dream yourself into a character; you must hammer and forge one yourself." — *James A.Froude*

"Character is much easier kept than recovered." — *Thomas Paine*

BUOYS

Buoys

A buoy is a distinctively marked and shaped anchored float, sometimes carrying a whistle, light or bell, and marks a channel or obstruction. We could think of it as something that is supportive, such as hope, courage or family and friends.

Buoys are not infallible, as they can break loose from their moorings, sink, or have their lights fail. We cannot follow them blindly; they must be used along with our chart.

Hope

"Man can live about forty days without food, about three days without water, about eight minutes without air...but only for one second without hope."
— *Hal Lindsey*

"Hope is the pillar that holds up the world. Hope is the dream of a waking man." — *Pliny the Elder*

"If it were not for hope, the heart would break."
— *Thomas Fuller*

"There is no medicine like hope, no incentive so great, no tonic so powerful as expectation of something tomorrow." — *Orison S. Marden*

"A leader is a dealer in hope." — *Napoleon Bonaparte*

"Hope is the last thing ever lost." — *Italian Proverb*

"Dreams, ideas and plans not only are an escape, they give me a purpose, a reason to hang on." — *Unknown*

"Hope in every sphere of life is a privilege that attaches to action. No action, no hope." — *Peter Levi*

Courage

"Man cannot discover new oceans unless he has the courage to lose sight of the shore for a long time."
– *Andre Gide*

"There is no substitute for guts."
— *Coach Paul "Bear" Bryant*

"Courage is grace under pressure."   — *Ernest Hemingway*

"Pain nourishes courage. You can't be brave if you've only had wonderful things happen to you."
— *Mary Tyler Moore*

"Courage is what it takes to stand up and speak. Courage is also what it takes to sit down and listen."
— *Sir Winston Churchill*

"The stories of past courage... can offer hope, they can provide inspiration. But they cannot supply courage itself. For this each man must look into his own soul."   — *John F. Kennedy*

"Courage is capacity to confront what cannot be imagined."   — *Leo Rosten*

"Life shrinks or expands in proportion to one's courage."   — *Anais Nin*

Family & Friends

"I have learned that to be with those I like is enough."
— *Walt Whitman*

"Lots of people want to ride with you in the limo, but what you want is someone who will take the bus with you."   — *Oprah Winfrey*

"It's the friends you call up at 4:00 a.m. that matter."
— *Marlene Dietrich*

"Hold a true friend with both your hands."— *Nigerian Proverb*

FAMILY & FRIENDS

"Don't walk in front of me; I may not follow. Don't walk behind me; I may not lead. Walk beside me and just be my friend." — *Albert Camus*

"Many people will walk in and out of your life, but only true friends will leave footprints on your heart." — *Eleanor Roosevelt*

"If you want an accounting of your worth, count your friends." — *Merry Browne*

"There can be hope only for a society which acts as one big family, not as many separate ones." — *Anwar Sadat*

"If you judge people, you have no time to love them." — *Mother Teresa*

"A friend is someone who gives you total freedom to be yourself." — *James Morrison*

LIGHTHOUSE IN FOG

Lighthouses

Who has seen an isolated lighthouse overlooking a high cliff with a vast view of the ocean and not marveled at its beauty? These structures, which have been used since about 800 B.C., emit a sense of security as they spread their lights to guide mariners to their destination.

Solidly built, the mere sight of a lighthouse gives us the feeling that no matter what we have been through, we will be safe now. Somehow, the beam from the light beckons and draws us in.

In my journey, I have come to view lighthouses as a symbol of faith, a belief in a Higher Being.

Faith

"For what is faith unless it is to believe what you do not see?" — *Saint Augustine*

"When you come to the edge of all the light you know, and are about to step off into the darkness of the unknown, faith is knowing one of two things will happen: There will be something solid to stand on, or you will be taught how to fly." — *Patrick Overton*

"Faith is the force of life." — *Leo Tolstoy*

"It is in our lives and not our words that our religion must be read." — *Thomas Jefferson*

"It is cynicism and fear that freezes life; it is faith that thaws it out, releases it, sets it free." — *Henry Ward Beecher*

"Only the person who has faith in himself is able to be faithful to others." — *Erich Fromm*

"We do not believe in immortality because we can prove it, but we try to prove it because we cannot help believing it." — *Harriet Martineau*

"Faith is not something to grasp. It is a state to grow into." — *Mohandas K. Gandhi*

"Take the first step in faith. You don't have to see the whole staircase, just take the first step." – *Martin Luther King, Jr.*

"Faith begins as an experiment and ends as an experience." — *William Ralph Inge*

CORRECTING

Correcting for Currents

On the high seas or open waters, currents can take you to unexpected places that you might not want to go. At times, these currents sweep us into what sailors call the danger lines of position. These would include adversities such as storms, regrets, fear, negativity and failure.

When encountered, currents of life, in this case, will cause you to reflect on certain values and to explore characteristics that are embodied in changing and correcting your journey's interruptions.

Currents: *A body of water flowing in a definite direction and which affects a ship's progress.*

Adversity

"If you can find a path with no obstacles, it probably doesn't lead anywhere." — *Frank A. Clark*

"A collision at sea can ruin your entire day." — *Thucydides*

"When I hear somebody sigh that life is hard, I am always tempted to ask, 'Compared to what?'" – *Sydney J. Harris*

"Obstacles don't have to stop you. If you run into a wall, don't turn around and give up. Figure out how to climb it, go through it, or work around it." — *Michael Jordan*

"You may have to fight a battle more than once to win it." — *Margaret Thatcher*

ADVERSITY

Risks

"To be alive at all involves some risk." — *Harold MacMillan*

"If you're not making mistakes, you're not taking risks, and that means you're not going anywhere. The key is to make mistakes faster than the competition, so you have more chances to learn and win."
— *John W. Holt, Jr.*

"To win without risk is to triumph without glory."
— *Pierre Corneille*

"If you play it safe in life you've decided that you don't want to grow anymore." — *Shirley Hufstedler*

RISKS

"Easy is not an option."   — *Les Brown*

"You have to risk going too far to discover just how far
  you can really go."   — *Jim Rohn*

"Most people live and die with their music still
  unplayed. They never dare to try."   — *Mary Kay Ashe*

"There's no such thing as a sure thing. That's why they
  call it gambling."   — *Neil Simon*

"Only those who dare greatly can ever achieve greatly."
                                                 — *Robert F. Kennedy*

Stress

"A life not put to the test is not worth living."
                                                        — *Epictecus*

"Life is not fair; get used to it."   — *Bill Gates*

"The tragedy of life is not death, but what dies inside
  while we are still living."   — *Norman Cousins*

"Work hard. Play hard. Live easy."   — *Unknown*

"No matter what the statistics say, there's always a
  way."   — *Bernard Siegel*

"We can't wait for the storm to blow over, we've got to
  learn to work in the rain."   — *Pete Silas*

As I say in my seminars, "Whatever you are willing to
  put up with is exactly what you will have."   — *Judy*

Opportunity

"Opportunity is missed by most people because it is dressed in overalls, and looks like work."
— *Thomas A. Edison*

"When one door closes, another opens. But we often look so long and so regretfully upon the closed door that we do not see the one which has opened for us."
— *Helen Keller*

"The successful man is one who had the chance and took it."
— *Roger Babson*

"We will either find a way, or make one."   — *Hannibal*

"How many opportunities present themselves to a man without his noticing them?"
— *Arab Proverb*

"If there is no wind, row."   — *Latin Proverb*

"Security is not the meaning of my life. Great opportunities are worth the risks."   — *Shirley Hufstedler*

"What is death to the caterpillar, to the butterfly is being set free."
— *Unknown*

Excellence

"We are what we repeatedly do. Excellence then, is not an act, but a habit."
— *Aristotle*

"Hold yourself for a higher standard than anyone else expects of you."
— *Henry Ward Beecher*

"The quality of a person's life is in direct proportion to their commitment to excellence, regardless of their chosen field of endeavor." — *Vince Lombardi*

"As in a game of cards, so in the game of life, we must play what is dealt to us; and the glory consists, not so much in winning, as in playing a poor hand well." — *Josh Billings*

"Example is not the main thing in influencing others. It is the only thing." — *Albert Schweitzer*

"Excellence is never an accident." — *Unknown*

OPPORTUNITY

SMOOTH SAILING

Smooth Sailing

Once we have adjusted for the unexpected adversity that the seas have inflicted upon us and for the mistakes we have made, we have finally reached a period of calm.

It's time to kick back and relax. Charles II, England's sea-loving monarch said,

"God will not damn a man for a little irregular pleasure."

I hope you have included some basic fundamentals for relaxation in your "ditty" bag. Navigators have, for centuries, kept essential repair items in these small canvas drawstring bags. Let's see what we have in ours.

Humor

"Common sense and a sense of humor are the same thing, moving at different speeds. A sense of humor is just common sense, dancing." — *William James*

"The kind of humor I like is that thing that makes me laugh for five seconds and think for ten minutes." — *William Davis*

"After God created the world, He made man and woman. Then, to keep the whole thing from collapsing, He invented humor." — *Bill Kelly, "Mordillo"*

"The devil made me do it the first time, and after that I did it on my own." — *Robert Fulghum*

"Warning: Humor may be hazardous to your illness." — *Ellie Katz*

"Humor is a rubber sword—it allows you to make a point without drawing blood." — *Mary Hirsch*

"And we should consider every day lost on which we have not danced at least once. And we should call every truth false which was not accompanied by at least one laugh." — *Friedrich Nietzche*

Happiness

"Action may not always bring happiness, but there is no happiness without action." — *Benjamin Disraeli*

"It is only possible to live 'happily ever after' on a day-to-day basis."
— *Margaret Bonnano*

"What we call the secret of happiness is no more a secret than our willingness to choose life."
— *Leo Buscaglia*

"Happiness is not so much in having as sharing. We make a living by what we get, but we make a life by what we give."
— *Norman MacEwan*

"Happiness is a conscious choice, not an automatic response."
— *Mildred Barlhel*

"Caring about others, running the risk of feeling and leaving an impact on people, brings happiness."
— *Rabbi Harold Kushner*

"Pleasure is the actions of the present, the hope of the future and remembrance of things past."
— *Aristotle*

Confidence

"Nobody can really guarantee the future. The best we can do is size up the chances, calculate the risks involved, estimate our ability to deal with them and then make our plans with confidence."
— *Henry Ford II*

"Experience tells you what to do; confidence allows you to do it."
— *Stan Smith*

"No one can make you feel inferior without your consent. Never give it."
— *Eleanor Roosevelt*

"Doubt whom you will, but never yourself."
— *Christian Bovee*

"Self confidence is the result of a successfully survived risk."
— *Jack Gibb*

Imagination

"We are what we imagine ourselves to be."
— *Kurt Vonnegut, Jr.*

"The true sign of intelligence is not knowledge but imagination."
— *Albert Einstein*

"You see things; and you say, 'Why?' But I dream things that never were; and I say, 'Why not?'"
— *George Bernard Shaw*

"Throughout the centuries, there were men who took first steps down new roads armed with nothing but their own visions."
— *Ayn Rand*

"I only hope that we never lose sight of one thing— that it was all started by a mouse."
— *Walt Disney*

"Live out of your imagination instead of out of your memory."
— *Les Brown*

"Without leaps of imagination, or dreaming, we lose the excitement of possibilities. Dreaming, after all, is a form of planning."
— *Gloria Steinem*

"Imagination will often carry us to worlds that never were. But without it, we go nowhere."
— *Carl Sagan*

Part 4: Port of Call

The hard work is over as you pull into port and drop anchor. It is time to begin again. I hope you have discovered abilities and strengths that you were unaware of having, and that you have learned a great deal from this journey. I wish you well in your new destination and remind you of the words of John Dewey:

"Arriving at one goal is the starting point to another."

Anchor: *Any device that holds something else secure, keeps it from giving way; anything that gives or seems to give stability.*

ANCHOR

Victory

"For a man to conquer himself is the first and noblest of all victories."
— *Plato*

"Victory at all costs, victory in spite of terror, victory however long and hard the road may be; for without victory there is no survival."
— *Winston Churchill*

"It is better to conquer yourself than to win a thousand battles. Then the victory is yours. It cannot be taken from you, not by angels or by demons, heaven or hell."
— *The Buddha*

"In reading the lives of great men, I found that the first victory they won was over themselves... self-discipline with all of them came first."
— *Harry S. Truman*

"Victory is sweetest when you've known defeat."
— *Malcolm Forbes*

"There are victories of the soul and spirit. Sometimes, even if you lose, you win."
— *Elie Wiesel*

"I do not think that winning is the most important thing. I think winning is the only thing."
— *Bill Veeck*

"Management is about persuading people to do things they do not want to do, while leadership is about inspiring people to do things they never thought they could."
— *Steve Jobs*

Wisdom

"By three methods we may learn wisdom. First, by reflection, which is noblest; second, by imitation, which is easiest; and third by experience, which is the bitterest."
— *Confucius*

"Wisdom is not a product of schooling but of the lifelong attempt to acquire it."
— *Albert Einstein*

"Much wisdom often goes with fewer words."
— *Sophocles*

"Every now and again take a good look at something not made with hands – a mountain, a star, the turn of a stream. There will come to you wisdom and patience and solace and, above all, the assurance that you are not alone in the world."
— *Sidney Lovett*

"Wisdom is often nearer when we stoop than when we soar."
— *William Wordsworth*

"One's first stop in wisdom is to question everything, and one's last is to come to terms with everything."
— *Georg Christoph Lichtenberg*

"We judge a man's wisdom by his hope."
— *Ralph Waldo Emerson*

"Everything has its beauty, but not everyone sees it."
— *Confucius*

"To acquire knowledge, one must study; but to acquire wisdom, one must observe."
— *Marilyn Vos Savant*

"The art of being wise is knowing what to overlook."
– William James

"Never mistake knowledge for wisdom. One helps you make a living; the other helps you make a life."
— Sandra Carey

"The soul is dyed the color of its thoughts. Think only on those things that are in line with your principles and can bear the full light of day. The content of your character is your choice. Day by day, what you choose, what you think, and what you do is who you become. Your integrity is your destiny...it is the light that guides your way."
— Heraclitus

"Logic is the beginning of wisdom; not the end."
— Spock, Star Trek VI: Final Frontier

PORT OF CALL

Success

"Success is to be measured not so much by the position that one has reached in life, as by the obstacles one has overcome trying to succeed."
— *Booker T. Washington*

"Success and rest don't go together." — *Russian Proverb*

"Facing it, always facing it, that's the way to get through. Face it." — *Joseph Conrad*

"The secret of success in life is for a man to be ready for his opportunity when it comes." — *Benjamin Disraeli*

"I've been polite and I've always shown up. Somebody asked me if I had any advice for young people entering the business. I said, 'Yeah, show up.'"
— *Tom T. Hall*

"Anyone who ever gets to the top of a field doesn't get there by him or herself. And once there, you should not forget the responsibility to help others join you."
— *Johnnetta B. Cole*

"Success usually comes to those who are too busy to be looking for it." — *Henry David Thoreau*

"Well done is better than well said." — *Benjamin Franklin*

"There are no secrets to success. It is the result of preparation, hard work, learning from failure."
– *Secretary of State Colin Powell*

"I couldn't wait for success—so I went ahead without it." — *Jonathan Winters*

"I've missed more than 9,000 shots in my career. I've lost more than 300 games. Twenty-six times I've been trusted to take the game-winning shot and missed. I've failed over and over and over again in my life. And this is why I succeed." — *Michael Jordan*

"How far you go in life depends on your being tender with the young, compassionate with the aged, sympathetic with the striving, and tolerant of the weak and strong. Because someday in your life you will have been all of these." — *George Washington Carver*

"Success is a little like wrestling a gorilla. You don't quit when you're tired—you quit when the gorilla is tired." — *Robert Strauss*

Closing Thoughts

Thank you for going on this difficult and long journey with me. I leave you with two of my favorite quotes:

"Help thy brother's boat across, and lo! thine own has reached the shore." — *Hindu Proverb*

"I don't know what your destiny will be, but one thing I know; the only ones among you who will be truly happy are those who will have sought and found how to serve." — *Albert Schweitzer*

For that, my friends, is what life is all about!

Lagniappe

SPOTTED SAILING FOR HOME

"Your ship was spotted off the coast this morning,
slipping silently through the fog...coming around the
cape, she appeared in a shaft of sunlight...and what a
sight to see! Glimmering as much as the ocean
herself. Massive and beautiful beyond belief! Laden
with treasures, happy times, friends, love, and...
Quick, you must PREPARE for her docking...you
MUST make space in your life for her gifts...
otherwise, just as quickly, she'll quietly slip back out
to sea."
—*Mike Dooley*

Endorsements

"What a terrific, practical resource for people. Taking precious moments to consider single powerful quotes from your book that have meaning for our own journeys can be a fantastic self-empowering resource to reach our own desired destination."
— *Dr. Michael O'Connor, Life Associates, Inc.*

"It is a truly inspirational book, which is thought provoking and very entertaining. I wish that I had compiled it."
— *Dr. David M. Warburton, University of Reading*

"The 'Quotes To Keep Your Boat Afloat,' ranging from Change to Success, provide a wealth of ideas for any leader, trainer or public speaker. Judy Suiter has provided us with views from the big window of life."
— *D.R. Wynkoop, Civillian, Department of Defense*

"This book was very timely for me. I have been at a major crossroads in my career/working life and have been considering a major change. A lot of older baby boomers are looking at another 10–15 years of working and are questioning what happened to their dreams (if they even remember they had any), and are asking if this is what they want to do for the rest of their lives. Your book may put some of them on a different path!"
— *Linda Pappajohn, SantoraBaffone CPA Group*

"Well written, easy read and a lot of quotes that make you say 'hmm'!" — *Alberta Lloyd, Coleman Management Consultants*

"Judy never ceases to amaze me! Her boundless energy creates a ray of light that bring joy and happiness to others. What perfect timing for this book. The first of the month is crazy at work, so I need 'Quotes To Keep Your Boat Afloat!' Best of all, is *The Journey* you take us on. It seems as if the quotes are on the sails, flying in the wind, taking us from shore to shore."
— *Claire G. Dugger, Southern Company*

"Great! Reading this book is like listening to the voices of the Masters, timeless wisdom tailored to our lives today."
— *Christiane Hoffmann, The Lilith Project*

"Another fine book from a fine woman...this list of quotes is fantastic. Quotes can be used for all occasions and can make the best points. Thank you for the wonderful compilation."
— *Jim Walter, Tyco Healthcare*

"Nothing epitomizes the best of Judy Suiter better than a book of quotations. Just as these quotes have inspired her, *The Journey* will inspire and motivate you to bring out the best in yourself and everyone around you. This is a must-have for your library."
— *Dr. Ira Wolfe, Success Performance Solutions*

"This is an embodiment of a feel-good-go-get'em book, a summation of life's journey from *real* and experienced leaders. It is more than a book of quotes; it is the culmination — *the essence* — of a leader's journey to impact the lives of others."
— *Kim Walton, High Resolution*

"I love quotes. I always say 'hugs are therapeutic,' 'smiles are contagious,' 'laughter is the best medicine.' This book stimulated my mind and gave me warm fuzzies."
— *Veronica Ross, Department of Defense (retired)*

"Judy Suiter's book on quotes is a great resource, as her selections help any speaker or trainer emphasize their learning objectives."   — *Bill Bonnstetter, TTI Performance Systems, Ltd.*

"Every great journey needs a great navigator. Judy Suiter plumbs the depths and scales the heights of understanding of, and affection for, the human condition. Reward yourself with her insights and vision."   — *Jim Cecil, James P. Cecil Company*

"I am amazed that these quotes have such power, whether spoken in our lifetime or echoing from history. I have found myself thinking — and later, acting — differently since reading them."   — *Roy Ramdjanamsingh, The Netherlands*

"One exposure to Judy will energize you for years. Her influence and character have helped me to stay motivated in difficult situations. More than one person has asked me how I stay so happy and energized over the years and I contribute it to one four letter word: J-U-D-Y."   — *Toby Tolbert, UTIL Automotive*

Additional Resources

from Judy Suiter

Energizing People—Unleashing the Power of DISC  explains Dr. William Moulton Marston's theory of behavioral factors in easy-to-follow language, so you can begin applying it immediately. It shows how to recognize and communicate with the different types, how to handle change and energy drains, how each type processes information, makes decisions and more. For readers who want to understand themselves and others, this is a quick yet complete introduction to how it all fits together, and how you can work more successfully with people for their benefit and yours!

Exploring Values—Releasing the Power of Attitudes,  reveals the "why" that motivates us to do what we do. This is the second in Judy Suiter's trilogy and reveals how motivating attitudes and values are developed throughout life, the six value clusters that have become the core for workplace incentive programs worldwide, well-known individuals who demonstrate these values in action, how to motivate others by understanding their attitudes and values, ways to appreciate and work more productively with people who have differing values clusters. Judy's great skill is making information accessible and practical to apply!

These books, as well as Behavioral Style and Motivating Values Assessments, are available from Competitive Edge, Inc. online or from the Associate from whom you purchased this book. Quantity discounts are available.

Additional Resources

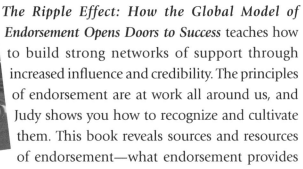

The Ripple Effect: How the Global Model of Endorsement Opens Doors to Success teaches how to build strong networks of support through increased influence and credibility. The principles of endorsement are at work all around us, and Judy shows you how to recognize and cultivate them. This book reveals sources and resources of endorsement—what endorsement provides for people, organizations, and nations, 5 elements that impact the level of endorsement, 5 steps to improving your personal and professional endorsement, ways in which endorsement leads to improved performance through the Law of Reciprocity, what causes loss of endorsement and how to regain it, and specific methods for measuring and raising your level of endorsement.

The Universal Language—DISC is designed as an encyclopedic reference manual for those who want to excel in their understanding of human behavior and practical applications of the DISC Model in their professional life. Now in its tenth edition, this amazing volume by Bill Bonnstetter and Judy Suiter, defines and explains how to learn the "language," applying it to work environments, using it in sales, and more—including explanations of validity studies, comparisons with other assessments, and more. This is a 285-page, hardbound textbook.

Competitive Edge, Inc. provides customized solutions to the people problems that organizations experience. We help our clients maneuver around human icebergs for clear sailing into the future, through leading edge technologies for team building, management development and candidate selection.